Help! I'm

Help! I'm 40

A Handbook for 39-year-olds
or
The Upsides, the Downsides of the Big–40

Clare Howard

Thorsons
An Imprint of HarperCollinsPublishers

The publishers have made every effort to contact holders of copyright work. All copyright holders who have not for any reason been contacted are invited to write to the publishers so that a full acknowledgement may be made in subsequent editions of this work.

Thorsons
An Imprint of HarperCollins*Publishers*
77–85 Fulham Palace Road,
Hammersmith, London W6 8JB

Published by Thorsons 1997
1 3 5 7 9 10 8 6 4 2

© Clare Howard 1997

Clare Howard asserts the moral right to
be identified as the author of this work

A catalogue record for this book
is available from the British Library

ISBN 0 7225 3382 9

Printed in Great Britain by
Caledonian International Book Manufacturing, Glasgow

All rights reserved. No part of this publication may be
reproduced, stored in a retrieval system, or transmitted,
in any form or by any means, electronic, mechanical,
photocopying, recording or otherwise, without the prior
permission of the publishers.

Contents

    Acknowledgements vi
1   Help! It's Not Really Happening 1
2   Help! I'm as Old as I Look 13
3   Help! I'm Not as Fit as I Used to Be 21
4   Help! I've Missed My Sexual Peak 37
5   Help! I Haven't Made My First Million 44
6   Help! The Children are Coming 56
7   Help! My Backpacking Days are Over 70
8   Help! I'm Part of the Older Generation 83

Acknowledgements

Thanks to all my 40-something friends for their insights into life at the beginning of their fifth decade.

Help! It's Not Really Happening

Small, But Perfectly Formed, Compensations About Being 40

You are just in time to discover what your parents meant by 'it's for your own good'.

You've still got those 15-year-old jeans in the wardrobe (because in a few months' time you'll have lost seven pounds and will be able to get into them again); you've now got a pair of glasses, which you hardly ever use – except occasionally (they *do* print the numbers in the phone books ever so small these days); you have a child who's struggling with difficult concepts like 'who is the real me?', and you

can understand (because, as a 28-year-old 40-year-old, you too, want to know who the real you is). Is it *really true* that you're on the cusp of the fifth decade?

It's Really True…

Take away the date of your birth from this year's date, and, if you are left with 40, then…it's true.

Most Common Male Reactions to the Above Sum

A) F***ing hell.
B) Oh, f***.
C) F*** me.

Most Common Female Reactions to the Above Sum
A) I just can't believe I'm *that* old.
B) I don't *feel* anything like 40.
C) Damn, I forgot to have babies.

Most of the above are interchangeable. It is not true to suggest that women don't use four-letter words.

> The best 10 years of a woman's life are
> between the ages of 38 and 40.

There are compensations, though. Years have a meaning. Groups of 10 do not, except that that's the number of fingers we have. Computer language – 'the language of the '90s' – isn't based on 10 at all. It's based on two. Thus:

$1 = 1$
$2 = 10$
$4 = 100$
$8 = 1,000$
$16 = 10,000$
$32 = 100,000$
$64 = 1,000,000$

So, look on the bright side, in computer terminology this book should be called *Help! I'm 101,000*.

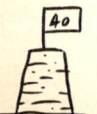

> You know you've reached your 40s when
> the only thing you don't want for your birthday
> is to be reminded of it.

Help! I Haven't got a Strategy

As the big day approaches it becomes increasingly important to develop a survival strategy. Are you going to:

A) Lie about it.
B) Celebrate with extraordinary noise and expense.
C) Ignore it.

Once you've decided which course of action is yours, you need to work out how to implement your strategy.

How to Lie About it

Your most important allies are, of course, your parents. They must be fully briefed, because you will, according to your new chronology, have…

Got engaged when you were 19.

 Taken your 'A' levels when you were 13.

 Left nursery school when you were 1.

 Gone to nursery school when you were minus 2.

You will thus have either to bribe or cut off all communication with your old schoolfriends, since they are bound to remember that you weren't a child prodigy in the lower third.

> 'I dread to think of life at 40' she said to her old schoolfriend.
> 'Why?' replied her friend. 'What happened then?'

How to Celebrate...

This is the bravado route. And can be most satisfactory for those who fulfil the following criteria:

 Noisy people.

 People with plenty of money.

 Those whose friends know your *real* age anyway – and it's time those friends shelled out for some *serious* presents.

How to Ignore it

This takes literally years of preparation. And involves not telling *anybody* at all – not even your parents – what your real age is.

You do have to be careful though, as adopting this approach means that you must never *ever* let your passport out of your sight, and never *ever* allow conversations to elicit more than one age-related

fact (you can say how old you were when you left school, or when you left school – but not both). It's a bit of a strain, but it might just be worth it if it's the right strategy for you.

> A man is as old as he feels – and a woman is as old as she feels like saying.

Help! It's my Party and I'll Lie if I Want to

To party, or not to party. That is the big question you have to face shortly after your 39th birthday. It may be that you decide to party prematurely, and celebrate your 40th birthday a year or two early. That way everyone is *amazed* by how young you look for 40 (which, of course, you do because you're only 37). This could all go horribly wrong if nobody said any such a thing, and all you've done is add unnecessary years to your age.

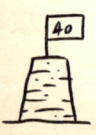

Doing it the other way round could be equally disastrous – as you'll realise when you overhear your friends saying, doesn't he/she look *old* for 40. (Which of course you do, being 43.) So, having decided that honesty is the better part of valour, you can either *Go For It*, or *Bury Your Head in the Sand*.

How to Go For It

1) Make a list of people who are very very close to you.
2) Add to it a list of people who are quite close to you.
3) And then add a list of people you know/might know/have known who are good fun at a party.
4) Send them all an amusingly self-deprecatory invitation implying that this is cause for massive celebration, and lots of expensive presents.
5) Extract a staggering sum of money from your bank account.
6) Book a restaurant/a function room/a hotel in the country.
7) Cancel the booking when you realise how much it will all cost.

8) Do it all yourself in your own home.
9) Wake up the next morning appalled at the mess, the expense, the enormity of your hangover and feeling very much your age…

How to Bury Your Head in the Sand

1) Don't let on to anyone, except those very, very close to you that the big day is approaching.
2) Insist that those very, very close to you take you somewhere hot, sunny and sandy for that secret day.
3) On the day itself, take yourself off to a remote part of the beach.
4) Dig a large hole.
5) Insert your head in it, and cover securely.

> Every time I look in the mirror, I find it increasingly hard to accept the fact that we were created in God's image. I just can't see God as being fat, 40, and wearing bifocals.

> *So you're 39 and you've screwed up – massively –
> carry on in politics.*
>
> By the time he was 40, Winston Churchill had
> been dismissed from the War Cabinet after the
> Dardanelles fiasco. But he carried on.

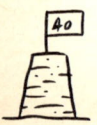

Help! I'm as Old as I Look

Small, But Perfectly Formed, Compensations About Being 40

The cosmetic industry is now so incredibly sophisticated that everyone can look Much Younger Than Their Age.

The 10 tell-tale signs:
1) You've reached a stage where the laugh lines have become crows' feet, and where your willingness to smile at the mirror to check this fact out has diminished with, well, age.

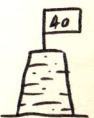

Help! I'm as Old as I Look

2) You look at friends/colleagues who you *know* are older than you, and are not completely convinced that you look younger than them.
3) You read articles about 'How to Stop Ageing' with extraordinary enthusiasm. Knowing they're not really directed at *you*, you nonetheless take those vitamin A, B, D pills the experts recommend.
4) You watch old films starring the idols of 20 years ago, and are horrified by how young they look.
5) You watch films starring idols of today and revel in the youthful good looks of the handful of 30-something stars.
6) You're increasingly appalled at the way journalists insist on reporting people's ages in every news story. It makes you even more determined not to be the (40-year-old) victim of a terrorist attack.
7) *His* distinguished high forehead has become a distinguished high nape of the neck.

8) *Her* sexy thighs have become the victim of orange-peel clichés.
9) You wear comfortable, practical clothes with expandable waistbands.
10) You flirt with people wearing comfortable, practical clothes with expandable waistbands.

Help! You're 40...

> I'll never forget the first time I discovered i was middle-aged. It was the day they showed a TV commercial for heartburn, nagging backache and greying hair – and I realised I was listening to it.

...but it's not necessarily the end of the world. Just remember:

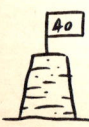

A) At least you're not 50.
B) You've grown up.
C) Lots of people look *fabulous* at 40.

People Who Look Fabulous at 40

Alec Baldwin
Isabelle Adjani
Bruce Willis
Melanie Griffiths
Kim Basinger
Michelle Pfeiffer
Richard E. Grant
Paula Yates (only joking – she's not yet 40)
Angus Deayton
Miranda Richardson

This is good news, after all, Sharon Stone is 280 in dog years; don't you wish *you* could cross your paws like that?

Five Bits of Good News on the Looks Front

1) There's a real chance you've got a little more money than you had when you were 18. So, though you may not be able to wear those thigh-high skirts/bum-huggin' jeans, you can at least afford a better cut of skirt/trouser.
2) You know that buttock-length hair/designer stubble doesn't suit you anyway.
3) No More Acne (but if you get a facial spot, at least it makes you feel young again).
4) You've found a dress style. It may be black and baggy, but at least you've made it your own.
5) Some people look better as they grow older. It could be that you're one of them.

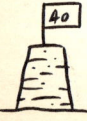

> When you reach 40 you make a fool of yourself in a much more dignified manner.

Most Infallible Ways to Spot the Approach of the Fifth Decade

1. Cosmetics

In this day and age 'cosmetics' is an asexual term. It's the '90s – one man can moisturise as well as the next woman. And one woman can *certainly* exfoliate as well as the next man.

There's nothing like an approaching '0' in the birthday to up the cosmetic investment stakes.

Five Ways to Spot the 40-something Cosmetician

1) A deliberate decision to upgrade their bathroom cabinet and spend at least another 25 per cent on each and every cream and lotion.

2) *She* – reads the comparative studies of anti-wrinkle creams with great avidity. And without really believing it *makes any difference at all* still mentally registers the most 'effective' make (purely coincidentally, the most expensive) and buys it the next time she's in Boots.

3) *He* – doesn't really have much truck with cosmetics as such, but does slap on the odd bit of after-shave moisturiser, does put on a higher factor sun-block – and looks wistfully at the bottles of 'Regaine' which seem to promise a bit of hairful miracle – at a price.

4) *She* – invests in yet more expensive tinted moisturiser, foundation and lipsticks and eye-make-up which distract attention from the skin.

5) *He* – doesn't.

So you haven't written a major West End musical – go write an opera.

Charles Gounod had very little reason to think he might go down in history as a composer – until he was 40, which was when he wrote *Faust*.

Help! I'm Not as Fit as I Used to Be

Small, But Perfectly Formed, Compensations About Being 40

People start to say you look good for your age.

It's a truth universally felt that the passage of years takes a physical toll. And at a certain point in life – normally around the age of 40 – you are definitely aware of the signs that you are not as fit as you once were.

Signs that You Are Not as Fit as You Were

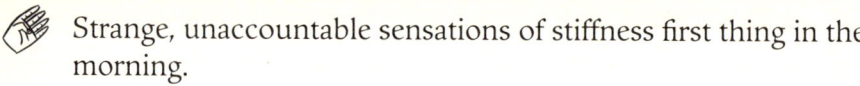 Strange, unaccountable sensations of stiffness first thing in the morning.

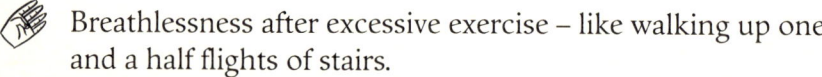 Breathlessness after excessive exercise – like walking up one and a half flights of stairs.

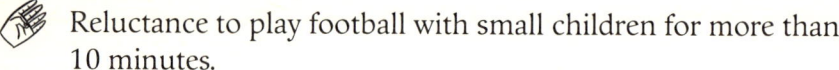 Reluctance to play football with small children for more than 10 minutes.

Distinct signs of increased bulk, which has nothing whatever to do with muscle.

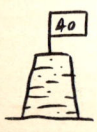 Inability to stay up until 2 o'clock in the morning.

Help! I'm Not as Fit as I Used to Be

 Back problems.

 Problems.

> The amount of years in excess of 30 is in direct proportion to the amount of money spent on fitness aids.

Help! I've Got to Get Fit

 Do you get more breathless after your weekly game of squash?

 Do you tend to cancel your weekly game of squash?

 Have you never played squash in your life – and don't intend to start now?

Help! I'm 40

 Are you fat and 40, or fit and 40?

This simple quiz will quickly establish whether you're heading for a heart attack or fightingly fit.

1) You've had a long, hard day at the office. You feel tired, stressed and have a nasty taste in your mouth from a little too much house red with lunch. On returning home you immediately:

 Have a large gin and tonic, a small cigarette and fall asleep in front of the television.

 Have a large chocolate biscuit, a small walk with the dog, and fall asleep in front of a fitness video.

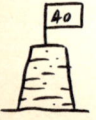 Have a slow jog with the dog, a quick bonk with your partner, and fall asleep on top of them.

Help! I'm Not as Fit as I Used to Be

2) Your friend has a flat at the top of 11 flights of stairs, and there is no lift. Do you:

 Have to catch your breath every other flight.

 Don't get breathless at all.

 Don't go to see them?

3) You see a friend (and contemporary) in running shorts jogging down your street. You:

 Whip on your own jogging kit and run after them.

 Feel guilty and shamed enough by their contrasting fitness and take the dog for another walk.

Draw the curtains and freshen up your gin and tonic?

4) Everyone you know seems to talk about little else but their morning session 'at the gym'. Do you:

 Despise them for only going once a week for half an hour.

 Feel guilty because you've only once been to one.

 Think they're talking about 'Jim's Wine Bar'?

If you scored 1(a), 2(c), 3(c), 4(c) then you're obviously a loveable hedonist, with a laboured sense of humour – and heading for a heart attack…

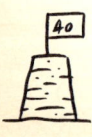

Help! I'm Not as Fit as I Used to Be

Help! I've Got to Get Fit Quick

So you've reached the age where you think walking is exercise and squash is dangerous. An age when the phone rings on a Saturday night and you hope it's not for you – because you're too busy trying to work out how to slot in the government's recommended 20 minutes exercise three times a week. Or you're simply too busy to work out…

…what you need is an *Instant Fitness Regime*.

An Instant Fitness Regime

1. Trunk Rotation

Feet shoulder width apart. Face forward, and without moving legs, rotate torso from the waist. Thrust hips in opposite direction to the twist. Repeat 15 times.

or

Help! I'm Not as Fit as I Used to Be

Trunk Rotation for the Less Fit

Place trunk, full of holiday clothes, reading material and clean underwear, in a parallel line with bed. Rotate 45 degrees.

2. Toe Touching

Feet slightly apart. Lock knees so legs remain straight. Reach for ground in front of toes. Straighten up to start position. Repeat 10 times.

or

Toe Touching for the Less Fit

Place partner on bed. Gently caress extremities of feet. Repeat as necessary.

3. Desk-top Press-ups

Stand back from desk, place hands on desk. Bend arms and slowly lower the body so that chest touches desk, straighten arms. Repeat 10 times.

or

Desk-top Press-ups for the Less Fit
Place right forearm on desk, clutching cup of coffee. Raise to mouth. Repeat until cup is empty.

Most Infallible Ways to Spot the Approach of the Fifth Decade

2. Wimbledon

To some, the annual tennis tournament held in South West London's All England Lawn Tennis Club may seem like just another sporting event. The 40-something knows better. To be even faintly aware of the Lawn Tennis Championships is to know that time is passing by.

Do *you* remember watching Evonne Goolagong beat Margaret Court? Do *you* remember watching tousle-haired Ilie Nastase clowning it up on the Centre Court, Jimmy Connors' romance with Chris Evert, Billie Jean King being a grown-up, as opposed to Andrea Jaegar and Tracey Austin not? Did you ever fancy Tom Okker and Adriano Panatta or Françoise Durr and Rosie Casals?!

Five Ways to Spot the 40-something Wimbledon-goer

1) They think one of the best men's doubles partnerships ever were Newcombe and Roche. Closely followed by Hewitt and McMillan.

2) They became quite fond of Billie Jean King and Rosie Casals, simply because they were older than them.

3) They remember Ken Rosewall and Rod Laver as proper old-fashioned tennis players, and regarded Borg and McEnroe as positive upstarts.

4) They fondly remember the Goolagong/Evert rivalry.

5) They are absolutely appalled to see that Stan Smith and Roger Taylor compete in the 'Over 45' doubles.

Help! I've Had All My Units

Average alcohol consumption per age group:

15–20
One glass of wine/beer/unit of spirits is good for you. Ten times the above, you discover, is 10 times as much fun. And you don't care what's 'good for you'.

Help! I'm Not as Fit as I Used to Be

20–25

Ten units after a hard day's work feels so good for you that you forget how bad the 11th makes you feel the next morning.

25–30

You start to worry about how bad the 11th unit makes you feel the next morning.

30–35

You're now really worried about how bad the 11th unit makes you feel. You're aware that you're not as indestructible as you were 10 years ago and regularly have less than 10 units a day.

35–40

You now don't drink at lunchtimes, except very occasionally on Very Special Occasions, and use driving as an excuse not to have more than three units in the evening.

40 plus

You're now practically teetotal. Or are you…?

Whatever they say about the damage alcohol does, *you know* that meeting people is fun, and even more so with a glass of something in your hand/down your neck. But you're not going to let it all get out of hand (except very occasionally, on Very Special Occasions).

For inspiration you look at those 40-somethings who don't drink at all, and then you think of Oliver Reed. And he looks all right on a lot more than three units a day, so maybe you could have Another Little Drink.

10 Reasons for Having Another Little Drink

1) You've got a new job.

2) You've been promoted.

3) You've been fired.

4) You've got married/engaged/decided to live together/have been going out together for a year/have had your first consummated date/have had your first date/have spotted someone in the street you really fancy.

5) Someone close to you is pregnant.

6) You've had your first child.

7) You've had your second child.

8) The third pregnancy is a false alarm.

9) It's your partner's 40th birthday.

10) It's your 40th birthday.

Forty? The secret of staying young is to live honestly,
eat and drink slowly, and lie about your age.

Help! I've Missed My Sexual Peak

Small, But Perfectly Formed, Compensations About Being 40

Sex is significantly better, you know what you're doing, you know what they're doing – size and formation doesn't count.

It's a much-written-about, and rather encouraging fact, that at the age of 40, the hormonal chemistry between the sexes is now closer to being the same as it has ever been.

Her oestrogens are dropping, as are his testosterone levels. Which means she's more orgasm-driven, he's less aggressive. That's the good news. The bad news is the 'M' word.

The Menopause: What it Means

For Her	**For Him**
Hot Flushes	Hot Flashes
Suddenly goes bright pink over dinner in that smart restaurant.	Suddenly goes bright pink over the waitress in that smart restaurant.
Baby Panic	Baby Panic
Haven't had them/ they play loud music.	Haven't had them/ they cost too much money.

Mood Swings
Semi-depressed and
needs lots of TLC.

Weight Gain
Increased water retention
results in increased girth.

Food Swings
Semi-depressed and
needs lots of BLT.

Weight Gain
Increased beer consumption
results in increased girth.

When a man gets to be 40, it takes him all night to
do what he used to do all night.

Help! The Naughty 40s

But…the beauty of being a grown-up 40-year-old is that you don't have to *pretend* any more. 'If at first you don't succeed,' as Quentin Crisp once put it, 'then failure may be your style.' On the other hand, all those years of practice may mean that you're really, really good at it.

So you can't beat your partner into submission –
go hypnotise them.

Anton Mesmer first looked deeply and hypnotisingly
into his patient's eyes – mesmerising them in fact –
when he was, yup, 40.

The other bit of good news on the sex front is that you're now old enough, wise enough and uninhibited enough to try something a little unusual. Or are you? Here are the upsides, and the downsides, of sex after 40:

Good News
You are old enough and rich enough to afford a house where there's privacy and space for an afternoon bonk.

Bad News
Your children are old enough, and mobile enough to find it.

Good News
You and/or your partner are now sufficiently advanced in your careers to go on working trips at home and abroad. This involves frequent ingestion of alcohol, and intense flirtation with friendly

colleagues of the opposite sex. Or the same sex. (This is a politically correct book, and you are old enough to do what you like.)

Bad News
Somebody will find out.

Good News – For Her
In a fit of depression you have decided that the menopause is nigh, you're unlikely to conceive, so don't have to bother with messy, dangerous or inconvenient contraception.

Bad News
You were wrong.

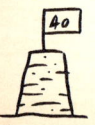

Good News – For Him
You have decided that your seat on the board, your Mercedes 600, your eight-bedroomed house, your half-share in a Tuscan villa

means that she won't notice your beer belly, your indigestion problem and your innate meanness.

Bad News

You were wrong.

Good News

Both of you know *exactly* what each other like; from fore-, mid- and afterplay.

Bad News

You're bored with it.

Forty – when you begin to feel like the morning after the night before – and you haven't been anywhere.

Help! I Haven't Made My First Million

Small, But Perfectly Formed, Compensations About Being 40

You are nearer the top of the waiting list for membership of the MCC.

Are your skills unrecognised? Are you frustrated, undervalued, depressed by youth being valued over experience? Are you short of disposable income? Are you short of *income*?

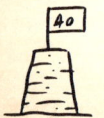

Don't worry, statistics categorically and undeniably prove that you are not alone. 71.2 per cent of the employed population feel the same way. 20 per cent of the rest feel almost as bad. And 90 per cent of the unemployed population feel even worse.

But that does leave 8.8 per cent of the employed population feeling pleased with themselves.

How to Spot the 8.8 per cent Who Feel Pleased with Themselves
1) They have large, expensive houses.
2) They have large, expensive cars.
3) They have large, expensive children.
4) They have a smug expression on their faces.
5) They are younger than you.

So you're not going to be the entrepreneur of the decade – invent a new religion.

Mohammed was 40 when in 610 AD he received a vision from God. The rest, as they say, is history.

The Complete A–Z of Financial Advice – Before and After 40

	Before	After
A)	A student grant	A mortgage
B)	Broke	Broke, but with a mortgage
C)	Can't get a part-time job	Can't get a full-time job
D)	Don't know how to pay for my round	Don't know how to pay for my mortgage
E)	Equal rights for all	Equity shares fall
F)	Future worries	'Futures' worries
G)	Guilt about debts	'Gilts' create debts
H)	House sharing	House hunting
I)	Income	Income tax
J)	Junk	Junk mail offering loans
K)	Knowing your credit limit	Knowing your credit limit

L)	Life ambitions	Life insurance
M)	Make mine a large one	Make mine a sound medical insurance policy
N)	Negative attitude	Negative equity
O)	Over the limit	Overdraft
P)	(Completely) pissed	Pension plan
Q)	(Quite) pissed	(Quite) pensioned off
R)	Racing debts	Racehorse investment
S)	Shared experiences	Share experiences
T)	Tessa (with the big return)	TESSA (with the big return)
U)	Utterly broke	Utterly broke
V)	Vac(ation)	VAT(able)
W)	Where there's a will, there's a way (with the birds)	Where there's a will, there's a way (and a lawyer's fee)
X)	X-files	Ex's alimony

Y) You only live once   You only live once you've paid off your mortgage

Z) Zen and self-awareness   Zen you get a bigger mortgage

But all is not lost. After all, Henry Ford didn't found the Ford Motor Company until he was 40, neither did Aristotle Onassis buy his first fleet till he was 40.

Most Infallible Ways to Spot the Approach of the Fifth Decade

3. Technology

Most 39¾-year-olds are only too painfully aware of the enormous advances that computer technology has made over the last decade. Those of them in gainful employment have learned at least enough of what's been going on to bandy words and terms like 'modem', 'CD-Rom', and 'Web site' with the best of them 20-year-olds.

But they're the ones who remember how long it took colour television to supersede black-and-white television. They're the ones who have children who could – for all they know – hack into the Barclays Bank database. They're still the ones who make mistakes setting the video and are totally mystified by the complexities of Super Mario Brothers.

Five Ways to Spot the 40-something Techno Baby

They can look up sales figures on their office computer, but if the screen shows anything even *slightly* unfamiliar they have to call in their 18-year-old assistant.

They invent increasingly unconvincing reasons for preferring to 'work on hard copy'.

- They buy the very latest personal computer/video recorder and are frightened by how their children don't need the manual to work them better than they can.

- They like playing solitaire on the computer, because they're sure it's improving their 'mouse skills'.

- They're increasingly alarmed by the complexities of the print-outs that rule their business, decide to go on a 'computer skills enhancement course', because, after all, 'knowledge is power' and they're beginning to feel they're losing out on both.

Help! My Career's Gone Phut!

It's bad enough that the managing director's 36, the finance director 31, and the assistant sales manager (the one they call the rising star, and the one all the girls fancy) has reached the ripe old age of 20. What you don't need to be reminded of is the fact that you've been working for 21 years, are the sixth oldest person in the company, and the fifth oldest person in the company is the subject of a lot of 'sell-by date' jokes. Is it time for a career change – is it time to dump them before they dump you?

Signs that It's Time to Dump Them Before They Dump You

The latest office move has deprived you of your corner office, and your new one is exactly nine feet narrower and you have to share it with the assistant sales manager's assistant.

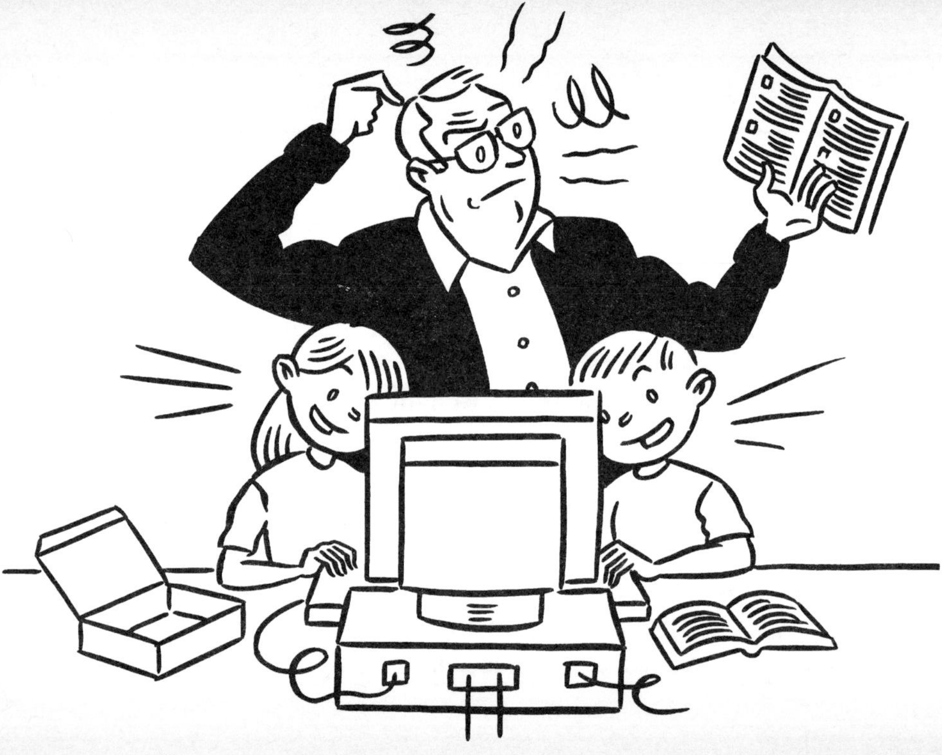

- The company has employed a management consultant, who shows a depressing familiarity with terms like 'downsizing', 'employee profitability' and 'early retirement'.

- Several senior people have recently left to 'spend more time with their families'. Which comes as a bit of a surprise to all those who know they have grown-up children at college.

- Your name has been mysteriously deleted from the minutes of the monthly meeting.

- Your name has been mysteriously deleted from the payroll.

Most Infallible Ways to Spot the Approach of the Fifth Decade

4. The Office Birthday

When you were in your first job a birthday was a bit of a laugh, and a good excuse to spend longer than usual in the pub with your work-mates. Maybe, if you were lucky, you got some particularly tasteless cards referring to your inability to have sex after your birthday drinks.

If you were even luckier, your boss would give you a bit of hard cash/a box of chocolates/buy you several pints. And everybody would say how much they wished they were *your* age, because you had 'your whole life in front of you' and 'just wait till you're 30, you won't like birthdays so much then'. Well, now that you're 30 plus 10, things 'are a bit different'.

Five Ways to Spot the Things That are a Bit Different

1) You start to dread other people's birthdays, because the subject of age *always* comes up, and it's then that you discover your new best friend in Accounts is exactly 12½ years younger than you.
2) You get more and more cagey about when your birthday is, because – although nobody likes being made a fuss about more than you – the subject of age *always* comes up.
3) You're relieved when your birthday falls on a weekend.
4) When they *do* find out that it's your birthday you're not very amused by all those cards which refer to your inability to have sex after your birthday drinks.
5) You are unable to have sex after your birthday drinks.

Forty is a difficult age. You're too tired to work,
and too poor to quit.

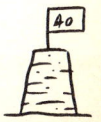

Help! The Children are Coming

Small, But Perfectly Formed, Compensations About Being 40

Your christening presents are antiques. Or, at any rate, look more like antiques at the car-boot sale.

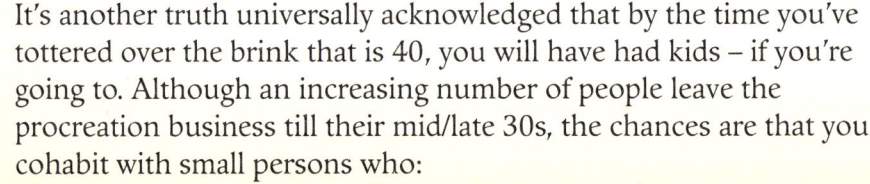

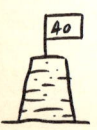

It's another truth universally acknowledged that by the time you've tottered over the brink that is 40, you will have had kids – if you're going to. Although an increasing number of people leave the procreation business till their mid/late 30s, the chances are that you cohabit with small persons who:

A) Have the family nose.
B) Have an extraordinary propensity for consuming your disposable income.
C) Leak.

As the recreation of self is arguably the biggest lifestyle change there could possibly be, it inevitably divides the Haves from the Have-Nots to an excessive degree. Their presence affects every area of your life. If you're a Have, you should – as Mother would say – count your blessings. If you're a Have-Not you should, as Mother would also say, weigh up the pros and cons.

    The following chart of the early stages is a handy reminder/checklist for the wannabes who've left it rather late, on the procedures and practices involved.

Stage 1. Conception

Pro	*Con*
It's good fun to practise.	It's good fun to practise (carefully).

Stage 2. Pregnancy (For Her)

Pro	*Con*
Luminous skin, air of smiling well-being, satisfyingly guilt-free weight gain.	Morning upchucks, worry, uncomfortable weight gain.

Stage 3. Birth (For Her)

Pro	*Con*
Unbelievable sensation of achievement, happiness and pride.	Unbelievable sensation of pain, fear and (possibly) a bit more pain.

Stage 4. Babydom

Pro	*Con*
Extraordinary and inexplicable pride, joy, happiness, fascination. Every single detail a source of pleasure.	Extraordinary and inexplicable belief that Something Will Happen to the Most Beautiful Baby Ever Born. Every single moment a source of worry.

Once the proud progenitors have done the deed, the hostage-to-fortune/lifestyle-change factors take over. And the Great Divide begins. The whole atmosphere of the toddler-run household is fantastically different to the (almost) adult order of the unchilded household.

By the time you've hit the Fourth Cusp, these differences are *marked*. As soon as you enter the 40-something childed household you'll spot them.

Guide for the Unchilded

How to Spot the 40-Something Childed Household

1) A small, irresponsible toothless person opens the front door, requests a present and/or tells you you smell.
2) The small person's parents (once pretty smelly and irresponsible themselves) smile indulgently at the toothless one before reluctantly turning their attention to you – and relieving you of your (very grown-up) bottle of vintage claret.
3) The toothless one's younger sibling makes itself heard upstairs. It is a mere five months old and wants you to know it is Still Awake.
4) The rather nicely decorated living room is positively *littered* with large pieces of brightly coloured plastic, and very old nursery rhyme books which look vaguely familiar (from your own toothless days) and very scribbled-on.

5) The rest of the evening is spent eating overcooked food in the company of a maximum of one parent, who has omitted to open your bottle of vintage claret.

How to Spot the 40-Something Unchilded Household

1) The door is opened, warmly, by a grown-up in extremely smart attire, wearing a plastic apron.
2) Your excessive lateness – due to the non-arrival of the babysitter – is greeted with a tolerant understanding of the gritted-teeth variety.
3) You have to carry the cot containing the youngest creation through rooms positively *littered* with highly breakable *objets d'art*.
4) The youngest creation reminds you that it is Still Awake at precisely the moment that your hostess serves the (rather delicate little) Italian starter. That you choose to attend to the insomnia rather than the starter does not go down well.

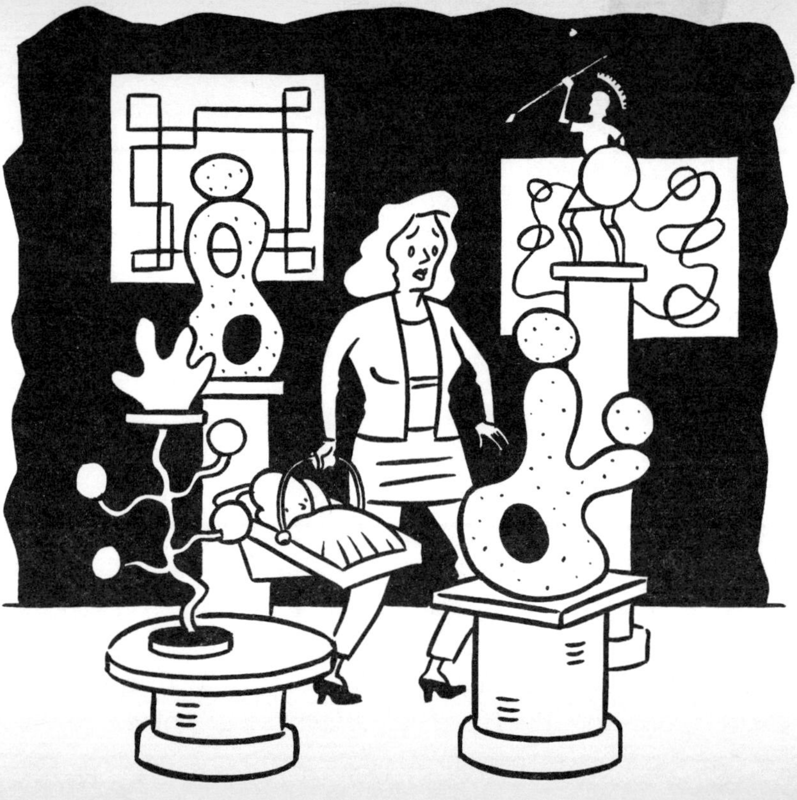

5) Your decision to leave early, having eaten little and drunk less, results in a cool farewell and an unenthusiastic discussion of how you must 'do it again sometime'.

> When we were 20, we planned for what we would do at 30. When we were 30, we planned for what we would do at 40. But when we reach 40, we plan for what we're going to do after breakfast.

It's not only the social life and the sex life that's terminally altered by offspring, it's also the finances.

It costs on average £10,000 to raise a 4-year-old child in the style to which you would like it to be accustomed, and a further £170,000 to raise it in a similar style to the age of 18. And by the time he/she has his/her very own copy of this book it will have cost you about £300,000.

But, hey, it's worth it, for a book as useful as this one.

> *So you're not going to be parent of the year –*
> *go paint a picture.*
>
> James McNeill Whistler had his first one-man show when he was 40.
> And Botticelli painted *Primavera* when he was 40.

The Teenage Years

Of course the be-toddlered 40-something is more than likely also to be in a state of be-teenageredness. Or at least to be in charge of a small to medium-sized person more than capable of being critical of its parents. Such a person has strong views on you, your physique, your lifestyle, your execrable taste in music, your amazing ineptitude with new technology, and your very, very tiresome obsession with tidiness. Their tidiness. It's in these areas that the responsibility of parenthood merges horribly with the awareness of 40-ness…

- *They* are terribly territorial about their bedrooms. It's Their Right to make a mess if they like, and to draw an absolutely sacred line down the middle of their shared room which their sibling – on pain of extreme torture – dares not cross. *You*, on the other hand, are incredibly grown-up – and are having a boundary dispute with the neighbours over the position of the fence and are the social pariahs of the street because you haven't mown the lawn or pruned a tree in years.

- *They* have suddenly become aware of growing changes on themselves and their brothers and sisters, and are Extremely Anxious that all dressing and undressing is done in absolute privacy. *You*, on the other hand, are incredibly grown-up and are horribly aware of growing extra inches/flab/girth, and are Extremely Anxious to avoid things like communal changing rooms and, in extreme circumstances, well-lit pre-bedtime undressing.

They are nervous about the new school, peer group pressure, whether they'll fit in, and whether they'll meet with their teachers' approval. *You*, on the other hand, are incredibly adult, have just started a new job, are nervous about the boss and whether he/she will approve of you, and whether you'll make any friends at school – I mean work.

They are particularly anxious to see the latest raunchy video that all their friends are talking about, and to acquire the newest, latest computer game that keeps all their friends up until the very small hours. *You*, on the other hand, being incredibly grown up, have just seen the latest Quentin Tarantino shocker, which you slept through because you'd been up the previous night trying to chainsaw the opposition/get just one more red five on a black six.

> 'Next week I shall be 40.'
> 'That's what you said a year ago.'
> 'Well, I'm not one of those women who say one
> thing today and something else tomorrow.'

Most Infallible Ways to Spot the Approach of the Fifth Decade

5. Christmas

When you were very young…I expect you believed in Santa Claus. You certainly expected to have a very nice time, and lots of presents, and too much to eat, and to have your parents be very, very nice to you and generally to feel it was, well, Christmas. Your main concern was that you had a bicycle/pair of roller skates/Spirograph/Fuzzy Felt like the ones they've got next door. You were completely oblivious to things like Tension, Jealousy (except if you didn't get a pair of roller skates like they've got next door) and whether or not it was the in-laws' turn or yours.

Now things are a bit different. You're mostly worried about how on earth you can afford a mountain bike/pair of roller blades/Super Mario Brothers like the children of the next-door neighbours. You're terribly aware of things like Tension (it's really the in-laws' turn, but you're not actually on speaking terms with them), Jealousy (the in-laws are jealous of your parents) and the fact that it's really the in-laws' turn. It's all a long way away from those carefree days of your youth.

*Five Ways to Spot How Christmas is Different
From the Carefree Days of Your Youth*

1) Now you eat too much Christmas pudding and drink too much brandy. Then you ate too many Twiglets and drank too much Coke.
2) Then you didn't have to worry about how much things cost. Now you do.
3) Then you didn't have to worry about January. Now you do.
4) Then you couldn't wait to get up at 5 am to open your presents. Now you just want a lie-in.
5) Then you looked forward to seeing Gran, now you wish you could spend Christmas alone in the Bahamas.

Help! My Backpacking Days are Over

Small, But Perfectly Formed, Compensations About Being 40

You don't need to apologise for not having been to the 'latest' bar/restaurant/club.

Does it seem a long time ago since a handful of lire, a slice of watermelon and a sleeping bag were all that was required for a happy holiday in Italy? Or one friend, one rucksack, and *The Good Beer Guide* enough for three weeks in the Lake District? Do you remember how walking round the ramparts/climbing a 500-foot mountain/ swimming two miles simply gave you a good thirst, rather than the sort of all-over ache that makes you worry about arthritis?

While it's probably true that nowadays you have no more disposable income than you did then, *now* you have to spend it on hiring camper vans, cottages or villas big enough to accommodate you, your children and the *au pair* (if you're lucky).

The whole concept of The Holiday has changed. *Then* it was about having the most fun for the most time for the least money, *now* they're an organisational nightmare which have to cost more money and take less time.

Holidays 40s Style – How to Spot the Difference

Skiing

Then

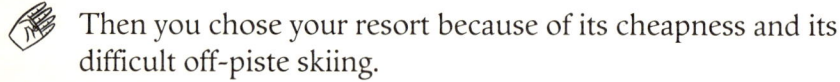

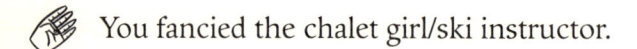

Then you chose your resort because of its cheapness and its difficult off-piste skiing.

You fancied the chalet girl/ski instructor.

You worked just as hard at the après piste as the piste, and were frequently to be seen gluhweining and boogieing till three in the morning.

You went home broke but happy.

Help! My Backpacking Days are Over

Now

- You choose your resort because of its cheapness, facilities for looking after children, and because it has lots of not very taxing green and blue slopes.

- You fancy the chalet girl/ski instructor, but realise they're more interested in your friends' 14-year-old.

- You come back to an early dinner and a few glasses of rough red, which make you feel terrible the next morning.

- You go home broke, exhausted, relatively happy – and surprisingly determined to do it again.

Camping

Then

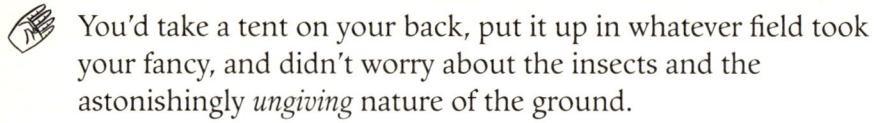

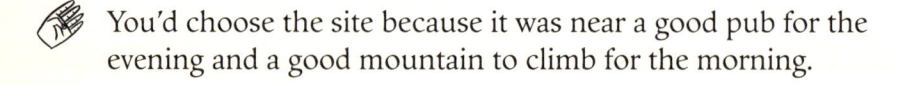

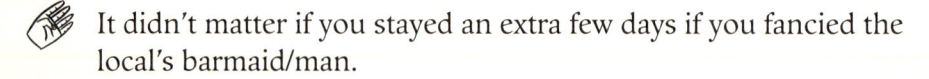

- You'd take a tent on your back, put it up in whatever field took your fancy, and didn't worry about the insects and the astonishingly *ungiving* nature of the ground.

- You'd choose the site because it was near a good pub for the evening and a good mountain to climb for the morning.

- It didn't matter if you stayed an extra few days if you fancied the local's barmaid/man.

Help! My Backpacking Days are Over

Now

You go to great lengths to find a camp site, at home or abroad, where there are proper loos and showers.

You take a special mattress to protect your bad back.

You only have exactly 10 days before you have to catch the train/ferry home because you have to be back in time for a sales conference/job interview.

So you're 39, too old for camping – go climb a mountain.

Sherpa Tensing Norgay was the first man to conquer Everest. Aged, yes, 40.

Villa Holiday

Then

You could be *extremely* picky about which three men and which three women were going to come with you. The criteria were simply based on who fancied who and whether you all liked swimming, drinking and playing tennis.

You chose a villa that was Abroad, not too expensive and had a pool.

You spent a lot of time deciding which of the three local restaurants you'd go to each night, playing Trivial Pursuit by the pool in the middle of the night, and – after too much Portuguese/French/Italian grape – would probably throw each other in the pool.

Now

Everything is planned way in advance: price, accommodation, availability, personnel, ferry bookings, flights, telephone contact numbers, exchange rates, local sights, whether or not there's someone to babysit, whether the pool is safe for toddlers – the whole expedition has become something of a Military Operation.

Your criteria for choosing your holiday companions is based on whether or not your children get on, and whether you can both get away from the office at the same time/afford the same class of villa.

You spend a lot of time organising each and every day. Who's going to take the car to the market, who's going to go to the beach, which restaurant you'll go to in the evenings, whether you'll have lunch by the pool or on the beach, whether to go on an outing the following day. (That part, at least, never changes.)

Long Weekends

Then

- The long weekend was sort of roughly Thursday to Tuesday, or maybe Wednesday.

- You went to the country, drove as far as your elderly car would take you without running out of petrol/breaking down. Any old B&B would do.

- Or you booked in for a dirty weekend in Paris or Amsterdam, because they were the best places to stay up all night.

- You enjoy yourself.

Help! My Backpacking Days are Over

Now

- You struggle to leave work on the 5.01 from Paddington or Waterloo and have a Saver return on the 20.07 from Exeter or Paris on the Sunday night.

- You have a precious (child-free) weekend-saver-special-valid-only-till–31-March deal in a grown-up hotel.

- You're so exhausted by the time you get there, you only have the energy to walk round the hotel grounds and then eat and drink far too much.

- You enjoy yourself.

Singles Holidays

Then

- You'd choose one friend, who you really, really think you can stand the company of for a month and a half while you take a train all round Europe/camp in Greece/travel round India.

- You meet all sorts of Interesting People on your travels, many of them of the opposite sex, and sometimes you abandon your friend while you make sure those people are as Interesting as you thought they were.

- You run out of money alarmingly quickly, have to ring your parents in order for them to make an extremely complicated arrangement with an obscure Greek/Italian/Spanish bank, so that you can spend another month meeting Interesting People.

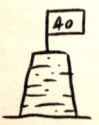

Now

☞ It is very hard to find one friend who you really, really think you can stand the company of for more than one week (because that's all the holiday you've got left).

☞ So you make a plan that involves a lot of other people, married or not, and is centred round An Event.

☞ Once you have bought the tickets for the Bob Dylan revival/opera in Bayreuth/Cup Final match in New Zealand, you run out of money, the Interesting People you meet know someone who is not only interesting but Extremely Well Off. In these instances the ritual post-holiday exchange of home addresses is more likely to result in an invitation to a private villa in Tuscany than it used to. Age has its compensations.

So you're not going to be traveller of the year – go find an ocean.

Ferdinand Magellan went round Cape Horn, found and named the Pacific Ocean on his 40th birthday

Help! I'm Part of the Older Generation

Small, But Perfectly Formed, Compensations About Being 40

You can say 'in my day' – and get away with it.

Help! My Vinyls Have Worn Out

…and not only have they worn out, but you have a broken stylus on your long-playing record-player, and Absolutely No Means of Replacing it. Gazing disconsolately at your dusty turntable (untouched for some years now by either your hand or your children's – heavens, they regard turntables like you regard wind-up gramophones. Or people who still talk about the 'wireless') – you realise that it's been many years since you played your EP of *American Pie*, *Gypsies, Tramps and Thieves* or *Bridge Over Troubled Water*. And from gazing disconsolately at your EPs it is but a short step to gazing in a similar way to your LPs…

The Incredible String Band (yes, you *do* remember them, indeed you saw them live), Jefferson Airplane, Carole King, Leonard Cohen, James Taylor, Joni Mitchell…where are they now? Where are *you* now?

If the children's tv presenters look young now, if today's tennis stars could be your children, if the *parents* of today's tennis stars

Help! I'm Part of the Older Generation

could be your children – then just look at the pop stars. They're almost as bad as gymnasts (all aged 12, and *you* remember Olga Korbut – now a contemporary of yours).

It's got so your memories of outrageously, excitingly new music are the nostalgia trips of today. Memories are made of this sort of thing…

Memories are Made of This (Sort of Thing)

1) You are at a supper party, your hosts don't want you to go (they've sent the children away to the in-laws, and want to play all night), they ask 'won't you stay, just a little bit longer?' The years roll back, the Supertramp tune goes round and round in your head.

TRUE/FALSE

2) A late-night tv documentary features a tragically early death, a sex god, a car – and it's not about James Dean. You immediately

think of a man called Marc, and 'Jeepster' by T Rex.

TRUE/FALSE

3) A TV advertisement against drinking and driving features a tune that takes you back to those summery days of drinking and driving. You realise that, to your children, Mungo Jerry might just as well be the name of a cartoon character.

TRUE/FALSE

4) Your nephew, or possibly your niece, has just gone to college. He/she is in a bedsit. It conjures up images. 'Bedsitter images'…

TRUE/FALSE

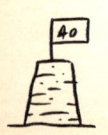

5) Somebody at the car boot sale, looking vaguely middle-aged and down at heel, is selling off their entire record collection: on closer inspection it contains titles like *Harvest, Tapestry, Let's Get*

It On, Just My Imagination, Lemon-Haired Ladies, A Salty Dog…and you realise it's *yours*!

TRUE/FALSE

6) You're feeling a little bit deaf. And a trifle spaced-out. And rather wet because it's been raining for the last two days. And talking of the last two days, that's about how long since you had a serious, uninhibited crap. But you're feeling very happy, because you have met the most wonderful bird/bloke. In short, you are not reliving life on a family campsite, you are reliving Woodstock…

TRUE/FALSE

7) You've just watched *Top of the Pops*. (Silly old you…) And it takes you back. To how it used to be. And from there it is but a short step to the madness that is remembering Simon Dee and 'Dee Time'.

TRUE/FALSE

If you've scored less than four 'Trues' in the above arduous test, then you either need a copy of *Help! I'm 30*, *Help! I'm 50* – or you should stick with the ageless attractions of Mozart and Beethoven or the equally timeless quality of tone-deafness.

Most Infallible Ways to Spot the Approach of the Fifth Decade

6. Television Programmes

There are those who only admit to watching television for the 'news and the nature programmes' (although they still seem to have an opinion on the latest shock/horror episode of *Brookside*), and there are those who happily admit to being Completely Up To Date with *Neighbours*, *Eastenders*, *X-Files*, and *Emmerdale*. Whatever your admitted number of television viewing hours, there is absolutely no doubt at all that nothing, but nothing, dates you like remembering

Val Singleton, John Noakes and Peter Purves (or, worse, Christopher Trace) as the *real* presenters of *Blue Peter*.

Do *you* know what they're talking about when the answers in the pub quiz night include *The Champions, The Persuaders*, and *The Man From U.N.C.L.E.* and – the original *Avengers*? Have you ever, in a mood of extreme and relaxed ebullience, started singing the tune (and All the Words) to *Champion the Wonder Horse* – only to discover that the entire assembled company is looking at you with pitying, 29-year-old eyes? Have you ever made passing reference to 'spotty dog', 'little we-ee-ed' or 'Andy waving goodbye' – in the happy, but completely misguided assumption that people know What You're Talking About? It's a bit of a giveaway, isn't it?

Five Ways to Spot a Bit of a Giveaway
1) You remember Mr Hudson and Mrs Bridges and all the other lovable folk in *Upstairs Downstairs* as if it were yesterday. Only

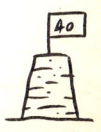

now they're re-running the series in the golden oldie weekend slot, and many of your friends have Never Seen it Before.
2) Whatever happened to Nyree Dawn Porter – *you* remember her as the glamorous Irene in the *Forsyte Saga*. (And it's been a long time since they repeated *that* on the golden oldie slot.)
3) You're only too well aware that Mel Smith and Griff Rhys-Jones', series 'Alas Smith and Jones' – has a witty title that is completely lost on its audience. *They* don't remember Pete Duel and Ben Murphy as two of the 'nicest outlaws in the history of the west'…
4) You think of Glenda Jackson as Queen Elizabeth I, and not as a Labour MP; you remember Richard Chamberlain as Dr Kildare; you can remember Dick Emery.
5) They re-made *I Dream of Jeannie* and *Hancock's Half Hour*. You remember the originals – 25 years ago…

Help! I've Painted the Sitting Room Yellow

How *boring* those DIY shops look when you're 20-somethingnotverymuch. But how packed with stimulation and fascination they are when you've reached the big four oh. Garden centres, kitchen showrooms and specialist tool centres…eat your heart out, Peter Stringfellow, *these* are the leisure centres of the baby boomers.

His Saturday afternoon in front of the big match on tv (surrounded by mates and empty tinnies); her Saturday afternoon wandering down the high street shopping till she drops (surrounded by mates and empty tinnies) – are things of the past. Now the high spot of the weekend is finding the right drill bit, the right curtain material and having a serious rub down (not) in the sitting room.

Then all you wanted was the coolest Che Guevara and Joan Armatrading posters on the walls, *now* all you want is a plain off-white sort of paint – the sort of paint that means you can wipe off the

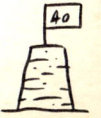

SALE

youngest's crayons and the oldest's cigarette smoke stains (it wasn't *him* smoking, honest, it was his friend).

Then you thought bean bags and a bare wooden floor strewn with Bob Dylan and Procul Harum LP covers was a 'stairway to heaven', *now* the stain-resistant carpet and the leather sofa bought in the January sales make the room look bigger, and will add to the value of the house when you try to sell it next year, because you need a bigger house to accommodate the third (unexpected) child.

Most Infallible Ways to Spot the Approach of the Fifth Decade

7. Meaningful Phrases

'Rhodesia', 'England's Tennis Champion', 'Winter of Discontent', 'the fickle finger of fate'…*you* know what they mean, but do they? The fact of the matter is that you can be having a perfectly normal conversation, with perfectly normal (except they're younger than you) people, when you suddenly realise that they are not only younger than you but they don't actually Understand What You're Saying.

Most Infallible Ways to Spot the Approach of the Fifth Decade

8. Politics

Do you remember the Oz trial, Harold Wilson's encouraging comment on the 'pound in your pocket', Vietnam when it was actually happening and the world's first heart transplant? Do you remember Alexander Dubcek, the three-day week and plastic bags with 'I'm backing Britain' written all over them?

Where were *you* when Martin Luther King was assassinated, Idi Amin expelled 50,000 Asians from Uganda and Reginald Maudlin had to quit the government?

Five Ways to Spot How Nothing Ever Changes in Politics

1) Then everybody was alarmed by corruption in the White House, when Nixon's Watergate was revealed. Now, of course, President Clinton is squeaky clean…
2) Then we were all horrified by the famine and deprivation in Biafra, now the world is well fed, and Rwandans and Ethiopians could tell you so…
3) Then the IRA threatened to bomb the mainland. Now, they have…
4) Then they were shocked by Princess Margaret's involvement with a divorcee. Now royal divorces are a standard feature of parliamentary question time.
5) Then they discovered a horrible and shocking cattle disease called foot-and-mouth. Now, bovine insanity has a set of initials attached – BSE.

Help! I've Forgotten How to be Cool

They say age is all in the mind. And your mind's gone. Or is it?

Time was, when driving at 105 m.p.h., jay-walking across Oxford Street, or climbing a 50-foot ladder were things you took in your stride. Accidents were things that happened to other people, mostly people older and unluckier than you. Or people low down on the billing on the Sunday night big film on tv. The ones where the sinister music and the bloody intimations of mortality should have meant they should have known better than to cross that road in front of Al Pacino in a fast car.

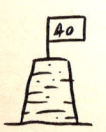

Five Signs that Your Phobias are Getting the Better of You

1) You look right and left six times before crossing a small country lane.
2) You go back to your parked car three times to check you've locked it.
3) You pay somebody else, anybody else, to fix that loose tile on the roof.
4) You don't overtake on the inside lane of the motorway any more, in fact you hardly ever overtake on the outside lane.
5) You unplug the iron when you go away on holiday, even though you've switched off all the electricity.

*So you're not going to be a world-renowned beauty,
get into politics – and cause worldwide trouble.*

'It's true that both Hitler and Stalin were in their
40th year before anyone took them seriously.'
Alan Bullock, Historian

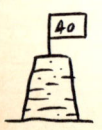

*In the twenties and the thirties you're just an amateur
But after you reach forty, that's when you become a connoisseur
Then it isn't grab and get it, and a straight line for the door
You're not hasty, you're tasty, you enjoy things so much more...*

Sophie Tucker

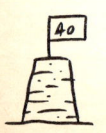